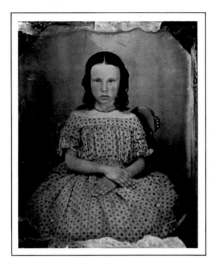

American Children

Springs Mills Series on the Art of Photography

The Museum of Modern Art, New York

Distributed by New York Graphic Society, Boston

AMERICAN CHILDREN

Photographs from the Collection of The Museum of Modern Art

Susan Kismaric

Exhibitions in the Springs Mills Series on the Art of Photography

at The Museum of Modern Art

Jerry Dantzic and the Cirkut Camera   May 9-July 30, 1978

Grain Elevators: Photographs by Frank Gohlke   November 6, 1978-February 4, 1979

Ansel Adams and the West   September 8-October 28, 1979

American Children   January 8-March 29, 1981

Copyright © 1980 by The Museum of Modern Art

All rights reserved

Library of Congress Catalog Card Number 80-84919

Clothbound ISBN 870-70-232-7

Paperbound ISBN 870-70-229-7

Designed by Nora Sheehan

Type set by M. J. Baumwell Typography, New York, New York

Printed by Rapoport Printing Corp., New York, New York

Bound by Sendor Bindery, Inc., New York, New York

The Museum of Modern Art

11 West 53 Street

New York, New York 10019

Printed in the United States of America

Half-title: Photographer unknown. *Alice E. Foh (?), Age 7.* 1860. Ambrotype, 2½ x 2 inches. Purchase.

Frontispiece : Lee Friedlander, *Anna, New City, New York.* 1974. Silver print, 7⅝ x 11⅜ inches. Purchase.

T

HE PHOTOGRAPHS OF CHILDREN

in this book are presented in reversed chronological sequence. Looking at them this way, as a pictorial record viewed backward through time, enables us to understand the ways in which photographers, like other artists, unwittingly reveal the particular spirit of their age. At the same time the movement from present to past evokes the memories of our own personal histories and proves doubly revealing.

Every child is a unique individual; unlike adults, however, children are relatively unpredictable and free from self-consciousness—although in degree this too will vary with the times. Nevertheless, several facts remain constant: no child has lived long enough to fully comprehend the dangers of recorded life, and no child's experience has provided him with the time and the space that gives one a sense of the past, of moments lost forever—or, antithetically, a sense of the future, of the inevitable process of aging and death. Unlike adults, children face the camera innocent of all but the present moment, and often with a startling purity of motive. In the varying degrees their eras prescribe both of these qualities can be found in all children's photographs, uniting the miniature adult-children of the past with their lustily independent contemporary counterparts. As a result children in photographs remain remarkably alike beneath whatever costumes and roles their disparate historical epochs assign them.

The photographers, however, who face these young subjects are adults. Each person behind the camera owns a fixed set of beliefs—his own and his era's—about the nature of childhood, and he portrays his subjects accordingly. It seems fair to assume, then, that photographers have always discarded those unconforming likenesses that inevitably must have turned up—those images that veered from the photographer's personal view or from the view of his society. While mid-nineteenth-century photographers sought in their young subjects an absence of feeling, their children mirroring innocence and purity, today's photographers would discard the same posed, idealistic representations in favor of images that express the individual child—and the photographer as well.

Diane Arbus, for example, whose portraits confront and attempt to unravel the mysteries of ambiguous individual identities, often photographed children because their feelings are so quickly and easily revealed. Her photograph *Loser, Diaper Derby Contest, Palisades, New Jersey* (page 21) shows us a baby oblivious to his recent status as contestant. His tentative expression, something between pleasure and pain, is clearly not a response to his failure to win the prize. Instead, his face, looking almost intoxicated, his shoulders, and his pudgy hands banged together fill the frame and topple toward us. The light of the flash creates a dark profile of his mother's head and arm, completing the backdrop of trees beginning at the lefthand edge of the frame. The pure egocentricity of his demeanor, combined with his inscrutable expression—is he going to laugh? to cry?—makes us realize that he, like any other baby, disregards our civilized concerns, our "winning," our "losing"; he's a *baby,* capricious, irrational, instinctive, and consequently always verging on the uncontrollable. Yet despite the mixed emotions aroused in us, or perhaps because of them, we cannot escape either his terrifying and compelling vulnerability, or more hidden, our own.

This contemporary view of children began in the period immediately following World War II, a time of renewed emphasis on family life. The affluent economy of that postwar period granted Americans a relative abundance of leisure time during which the events of family life (gatherings, holy communions, graduations) became subjects for not only the amateur photographer, but for the serious, artistic one as well. With a growing sophistication regarding the possibilities of their medium, photographers began making pictures of children that portrayed a new type of personal ambition and revealed new stylistic interests. The result was a profusion of increasingly personal photographic descriptions of individual children. Photographs from the 1950s and 60s, for example, show children in the backyard, the bedroom, and the kitchen.

At the same time the influence of television, "instant" cameras, and home movies gave children a growing awareness of their self-images. Photographers turned this to their own advantage, occasionally even making the child's response to being photographed the subject of the photograph. For example in Ken Josephson's picture (page 35) the boy raises his arms in imitation of the photographer, whose raised arms we see in shadow. The boy shoots a toy gun while the photographer "shoots" a camera. In this photograph of a child's spontaneous reaction to the process of picture-making we are reminded of the way children learn, by imitating adult gestures.

In contemporary photographs the adolescent is also seen in a new way. Adolescent sexuality, for example, has a new pictorial frankness. In both Diane Arbus's and Emmet Gowin's photographs of adolescent couples (pages 24 and 34 respectively) we are shown the beginnings of the male/female bond that presages their future and reveals the photographer's acknowledgment of young, burgeoning sexuality; in both photographs the young boys attempt the postures of grown men, wrapping their arms around the girls in possession and protection. To make a further point, Gowin posed his couple before an automobile, the American symbol of social liberty, of teenage sexual opportunity.

Many contemporary photographers are interested in the complexities of youth because society itself is fascinated with youth, with prolonging it for both economic and aesthetic reasons. With longer lifespans and less economic strain, the young can postpone the responsibilities of establishing a career and family, and are freer to create their identities on their terms. At the same time the adult, too, is freer to redefine his identity, and this often involves a concern with staying young. With the values of youth and adulthood less clearly defined, we continuously blur the distinctions between child, adolescent, and adult, each group assuming the qualities and experiences of the others.

Yet photographing children remains special, for children still live out their fantasies as part of their reality, and sensitive adult photographers share this proclivity. Because they keep alive the child in themselves, they understand and can capture the elements of fantasy in the child's subtle and fleeting array of gestures and movements. In the 1940s Helen Levitt, then in her twenties, managed this task superbly. She entered the fantasy world of children playing on the streets of New York and created from it a body of pictures that captures more of the nature of childhood than any made previously. Her work reminds us that there is a separation between adults and children: adults generally present themselves in socially accepted ways, with predictable handshakes, pats on the back, and quick, false smiles, while children usually do not. They are just as likely to casually flop over, play dead, stand on one foot, or run away. Their self-absorption eliminates their self-observation, revealing a type of self-direction and autonomy known only to those whose fantasies are central to their daily life: children, eccentrics, psychotics.

Thus in the Levitt photograph on page 47 we see three young boys living the drama of cops and robbers. With the life-and-death intensity of the hunted they take cover behind the wall of a stoop. One cowers in a corner as the other two, with an almost balletic precision, precariously balance at the edge of the step, searching in terror for their enemy. Levitt's recognition of the terrible seriousness of child's play was her central talent, a result perhaps of her own recent passage from childhood. Whatever the reason, her sure instincts led her to understand the significance of play in children's lives and to capture it in her photographs.

Helen Levitt's pictures were among the first in this country in the genre that would later be labeled "street photography." Clearly the miniature camera, introduced some twenty years before, proved invaluable to photojournalists, enabling them to make pictures easily, quickly, and with a minimum of equipment. This crucial technical advance also provided the potential for new aesthetic possibilities. The smaller camera and faster film allowed photographers to take pictures of people and events during the daily unfolding of life. Gestures, encounters, and relationships that previously had not been considered material for the serious photographer took on importance and meaning, resulting in the street photography of the 1940s.

During the first half of the 1940s America was at war. For those photographers who were not photojournalists, who did not photograph the war or its consequences, and who were interested in expressing their feelings about the world, the streets of the cities provided the raw material for a wealth of photographs based on small dramas and gestures. As always with city children, and perhaps more so during this time, the street was their backyard; it was there that Levitt and others sought to capture the spontaneity of children.

In photographs taken a decade earlier, during the Depression, children were frequently seen as witnesses to tragedy. As John Updike has written in a *New Yorker* piece, "Children in their brutal frankness dramatize the socio-economic secrets of a place."* Photographers, enlisted by the Farm Security Administration to record the life of people in rural areas of the United States so that their desperate condition could be made clearer to city dwellers and government officials, saw children as eloquent embodiments of the plight of migrant workers, displaced families, and drought victims. The Depression vividly showed us, a nation with a brief history, the inequities of our imperfect system, and pictures of children powerless against their pain reflected their parents' condition as well as magnified it.

Dorothea Lange's 1930 portrait of a damaged child (page 55) is a visual record of the worst of secrets, America's inability to prevent the injustice of a bad economy from destroying lives. As the young girl stands in front of a wall pieced from tin she looks directly into the camera with no visible response to the photographer. Firmly centered in the picture, she stands draped in a filthy makeshift dress, confronting us with hard eyes that match the metal wall. She appears to be lost forever to ordinary human contact. The power of the Farm Security Administration photographs is in their description of banishment, which evokes a universal terror of exile from society.

A decade before that time of great deprivation, during the affluent period that followed World War I, Freud's contributions to an understanding of the true nature of childhood might have provided the impetus for more personal descriptions of children; however not until several decades later would his ideas become integrated into our perception of childhood. After World War I many gifted American photographers, like the writers and painters of the 1920s, left the United States to pursue the life of the artist. For many artists the quest for freedom of self-expression often required an independence from the mundane responsibilities and intimacies of family life. Among them was Edward Weston, who in 1921 met Tina Modotti, an actress and model of great beauty (and later a photographer); two years later he left his wife and four sons to pursue his art and to live with Tina in Mexico.

Weston made the two photographs of his son Neil (pages 62, 63) during a return visit to his family in California in 1925. For Weston and other photographers of this period artistic

---

*John Updike, "Dark Smile, Devilish Saints," *The New Yorker,* August 11, 1980, pp. 82-89.

photographic activity meant a concern with subjects that had been selected mainly in order to demonstrate certain problems of form. In *Neil Asleep*, for example, the faceless boy lies sprawled on a couch, unanchored, seeming to float against the velvet backdrop. The angles of his limbs create a delicate natural pattern, with his relaxed body contrasted against the sharply defined textures of his corduroy pants and the couch. The emphasis here is not on human relationships, but on aesthetics.

Earlier still in the nation's history, several disparate ambitions and intentions of Americans, particularly of American artists, can be seen in the work of two very different groups of photographers: the reformers and the aestheticians. Photographs of American children taken during the late nineteenth to the early twentieth century reveal contrasting ideas about the nature and use of the photographic medium, and indicate as well changes in the way Americans saw their young. The industrialization and urbanization of the 1860s left us with the new evils of technology. Children, no longer needed on the farms, left in droves for the factories in the cities, joining the children of immigrant families to form a child labor force. No governing agency protected their welfare. As a result children worked brutally long hours with little financial reward and under conditions that were unhealthy both physically and psychologically. Some photographers of the period used their art to provoke society's conscience and to cry for changes. Foremost among these were the documentary photographers Jacob Riis and Lewis Hine, two great social reformers.

This group of justice-seekers is best exemplified by Jacob Riis, an immigrant from Denmark. Arriving in New York City during a period of economic decline, he, like many of his fellow emigrés, spent his first years in America in a desperate search for work. His previous newspaper experience in his native country led him, in 1877, to become a police reporter for the New York *Tribune* and the Associated Press. The evils he saw during this period roused his social conscience and he became a muckraker, using his writing and photography to expose corrupt politicians and landlords whose greed resulted in over-crowded tenements, crime-ridden slums, and scores of homeless children. Riis brought widespread public attention to these collective ills through his photographs and writing; and his book *How the Other Half Lives*, eventually published in 1890, helped win government reform. Thus Riis became the first American photographer to understand the power of photography as a formidable weapon for social change.

Riis's photographic technique was simple and direct. He walked the tenement area streets and alleys in search of the most graphic examples of their atrocities. Often using flash powder to light these dismal scenes, he took pictures that bear the stark and persuasive force of fact. The children in Riis's photographs, like the children on page 72, often appear old beyond their years and hopelessly trapped in a hostile world that is beyond their control.

Although Riis and Lewis Hine shared a belief that photography could effectively be used for propaganda, a comparison of their pictures points up the difference in their attitudes. Whereas Riis, the muckraker, used his camera to expose the selfishness of others, Hine emphasized instead the inviolate human dignity of his subjects, their spiritual nobility despite their obviously harsh deprivations. From 1908 to about 1918 Hine made photographs for the National Child Labor Committee to aid their legislative battle against the exploitation of children. His photographs show children who suffer but do not succumb; rather, they demonstrate their inherent goodness and strength. In contrast Riis portrays children as utter victims. By photographing children from their own height, so that they could look directly into the camera, Hine allowed his subjects a larger presence, a larger humanity, without a hint of condescension. The young boy in Hine's photograph on page 67 stands with an almost alarming self-confidence, smoking a cigar, a bit overwhelmed by his bicycle but nonetheless exhibiting an admirable resilience of character. Different though they were, Riis and Hine, using photography in their separate ways to document the conditions they deplored, proved able to alter social conditions.

At the same time in American history a second group of photographers emerged: the pictorialists and Photo-Secessionists, whose concern was with pure aesthetics. After the Civil War American photographers had investigated the vast lands of their continent using the large-format camera, which required cumbersome glass plates and unwieldy equipment, to make photographic surveys of the uncharted West. Not until the invention of the Kodak roll film camera in 1888 did amateurs and the general public have the means to make their own photographs. And from the ranks of these new amateur photographers and hobbyists emerged several whose dawning understanding of the medium led them to believe that a photograph might be more than a document, that it might say something more creative. The best and most serious of these practitioners, led by Alfred Stieglitz, formed the Photo-Secession, a society created to promote, through exhibitions and publications, standards of artistic photography. Firm in their insistence that photography was a fine art, they made photographs that often resembled paintings. Using elaborate printing techniques, they created works that did indeed conform to one classic definition of art, "a thing of form and beauty," while ignoring the potential of the camera to record other aspects of their world.

The members of the Photo-Secession took as their subject matter the people and everyday objects of their lives, but transformed them into artistic works bearing timeless symbolic meaning. In Gertrude Käsebier's *Adoration* (page 71) the woman and baby resemble the madonna and child of a sixteenth-century painting. The peaceful, naked baby stretches from his mother's lap as she sits in flowing gown wearing the expression of a saintly and patient Mary. Even the symbolic weight of the title suggests an eternal and boundless love on the part of all mothers for all their children.

Another example is John G. Bullock's 1896-98 portrait of a boy and girl fishing, *Young Anglers* (page 77). The bank of a gentle river beneath a large old tree provides an idyllic setting, far from the dirty, clamorous and unhealthy city, for the young girl dressed in white pinafore who stands stiffly and patiently awaiting her fish. With the same commitment to their mutual endeavor, her male counterpart lies on the grass in this peaceful, bucolic scene.

Like many in the Photo-Secessionists' photographs of children, these young subjects, presented within beautiful constructions, seem inviolable and in complete harmony.

Similarly, Doris Ulmann's precisely balanced *Portrait of a Young Boy* (page 65) provides a vestigial image of idealized nineteenth-century youth. Although the specific date and locale are uncertain, we know that Ulmann worked in Appalachia and the South from 1911 until 1925. Despite his worn overalls and tattered sweater, the drinking cup testifying to the outdoor workers' long and hard hours, he is not a victim of that work. Rather, he is testimony to the benefits of country life. The shyness he retains prevents him from looking directly into the camera. With his expression of tranquility and patience, while gently cupping a recently plucked apple in his hand, he stands balanced between planks of wood as though he were waiting to emerge, to become more a part of this world.

In the work of the Photo-Secessionists we perceive a yearning for a less complicated time. By joining in their imagery the innocence of nature with the innocence of children, they offer a romanticized view of the world that is in direct antithesis to the harsher, documentary visions of Riis and Hine.

In 1839, when photography was introduced to America, it had a practical use. The daguerreotypes, tintypes, and ambrotypes of the 1840s, 50s, and 60s provided inexpensive replicas of the person photographed. Children photographed during this period embody the Victorian ideals of their parents. It was not possible to capture the spontaneity of childhood in photographs taken in midcentury. The relatively long exposures required meant that a child's natural tendency to move had to be restrained. As a result, with their stiff postures, children in photographs resemble small adults. In the photograph *Alice Foh(?)* on page 70 the little girl sits with her hands awkwardly folded in her lap. The collaboration between the photographer and child apparently was at a minimum, having more to do with the commercial pressures exerted by the parent-client than with a spontaneous meeting of photographer and subject. The approach to the subject had probably been decided upon before the photographic session, and the demands of the client did not allow room for anyone's imagination. Yet undesired elements are recorded. The eyes of the little girl reveal fear, anger, or perhaps simple noncomprehension. For then, as always, children were photographed whether or not they wanted to be.

In photographs a child, like an adult, is described and revealed through a visual record of his presence in the world. It would seem, then, that since photographs describe these physical aspects they might capture something of the true nature of the child in his language of gesture, the vocabulary of his complexity. Yet the photographer, endowed with all the knowledge gained during his own passage to and through adulthood, cannot help but see the child as a metaphor for his own experience. Thus the photograph is more than a description of a child: it also becomes a metaphor of adulthood. Our response to it touches our most intimate feelings, for our personal histories are always with us.

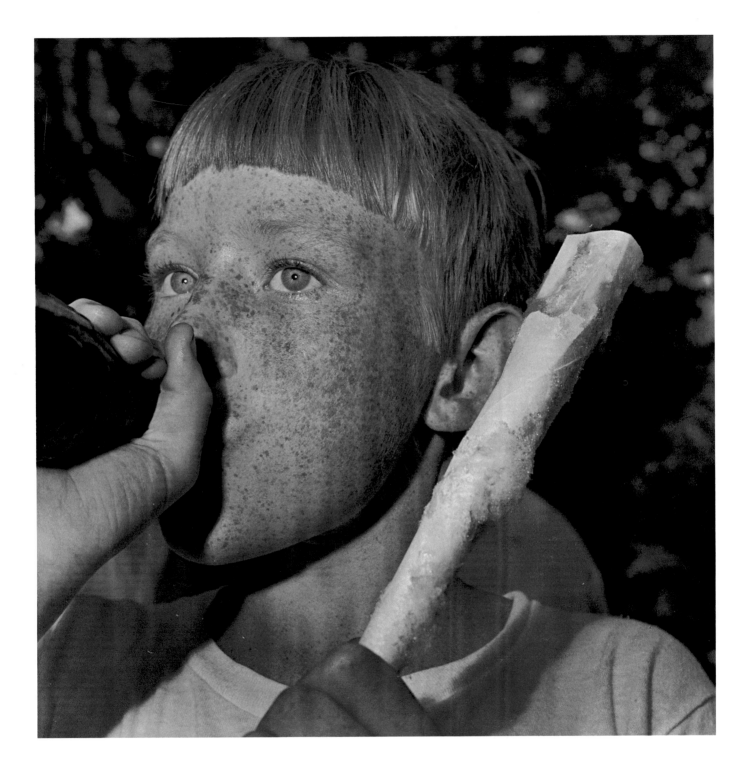

ROSALIND SOLOMON

Boy with Cotton Candy. First Mondays, Scottsboro, Alabama. 1976
14⅞ x 14¹⁵⁄₁₆ inches. Gift of the photographer

BRUCE HOROWITZ

Untitled. 1977
13⁹⁄₁₆ x 13⁹⁄₁₆ inches. Gift of the photographer

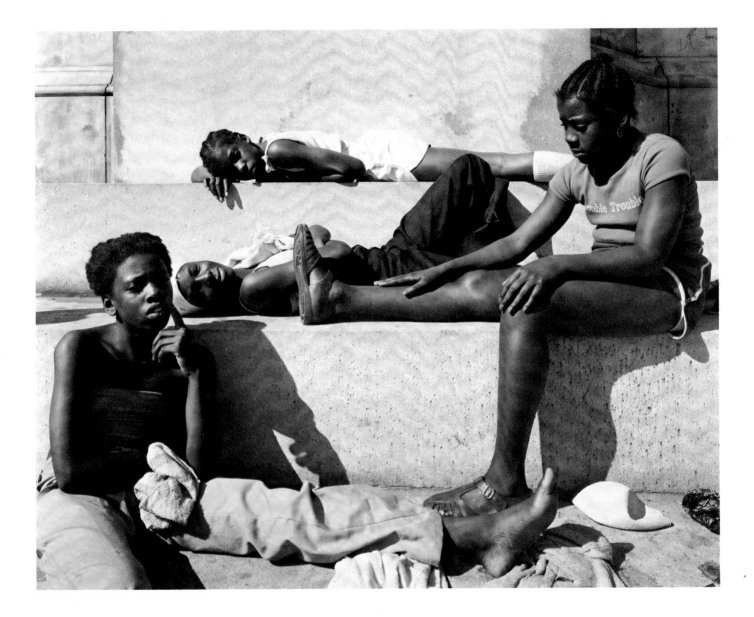

NICHOLAS NIXON

Boston Common. 1978
7⅝ x 9⅝ inches. Gift of the photographer

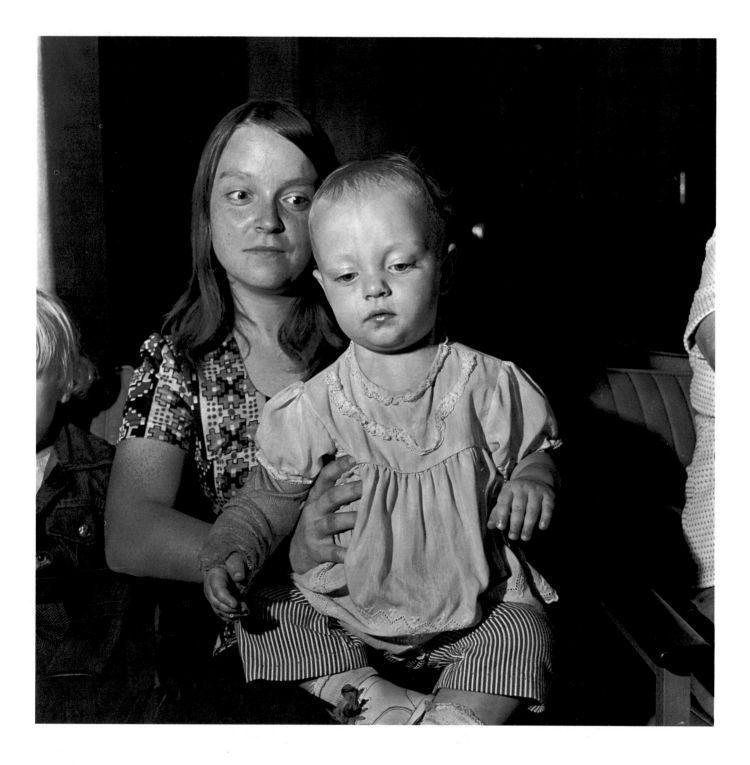

ROSALIND SOLOMON

Hospital Series. Erlanger Hospital. Chattanooga, Tennessee. 1975
15⅜ x 15¼ inches. Gift of the photographer

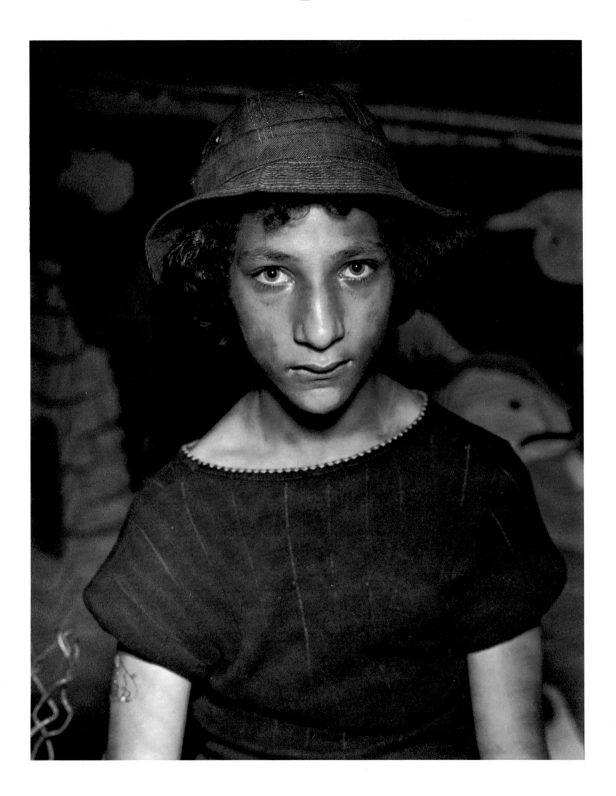

JERRY THOMPSON

Coney Island. 1973
9⅞ x 8 inches. Joseph G. Mayer Fund

MARK GOODMAN

Donald York, Jr., Standing Beside His Father's Wrecker, July 4, 1974
9³⁄₁₆ x 13⅛ inches. Purchase

DIANE ARBUS

Child with Toy Hand Grenade. 1962
8⅜ x 7¼ inches. Purchase

DIANE ARBUS

Loser, Diaper Derby Contest, Palisades, New Jersey. 1967
15 x 14½ inches. Gift of the photographer

CHAUNCEY HARE

Kitchen, Kensington, California. 1968
8⁷⁄₁₆ x12⅛ inches. Purchase

BRUCE HOROWITZ

Russian Man with his Grandson on the First Sunny Day
of a Long Winter. 1973
10¼ x 10½ inches. Gift of the photographer

DIANE ARBUS

Teenage Couple on Hudson Street, New York City. 1963
14¾ x 14⅞ inches. Purchase

EMMET GOWIN

Barry and Dwayne, Danville. 1969
5¼ x 6⅞ inches. Anonymous Fund

YASUHIRO ISHIMOTO

Boy with Starry Mask, Chicago. 1960
6¹¹/₁₆ x 9⁵/₁₆ inches. Gift of the photographer

DON WIGHT

Brigitta. 1965
7⅝ x 9⅞ inches. Benjamin Zeller Memorial Fund

LARRY FINK

Before the Confirmation. 1962
6⅜ x 8⅞ inches. Purchase

KEN HEYMAN

Willie. July, 1959
9⅜ x 7 inches. Gift of the photographer

GEORGE KRAUSE

Untitled. Philadelphia. 1962
6⅛ x 4³⁄₁₆ inches. Purchase

GEORGE KRAUSE

Untitled. Philadelphia. 1960
4¾ x 7 inches. Purchase

SIMPSON KALISHER

Untitled. 1963
13½ x 9 inches. Gift of the artist in memory of Ben Schultz

EMMET GOWIN

Danville, Virginia. 1966
4⁵⁄₁₆ x 5½ inches. Purchase

KEN JOSEPHSON

Bradley, Honolulu. 1968
6 x 9 inches. Purchase

DAVE HEATH

Untitled. From "A Dialogue with Solitude," #5, New York, 1960
9¾ x 6½ inches. Purchase

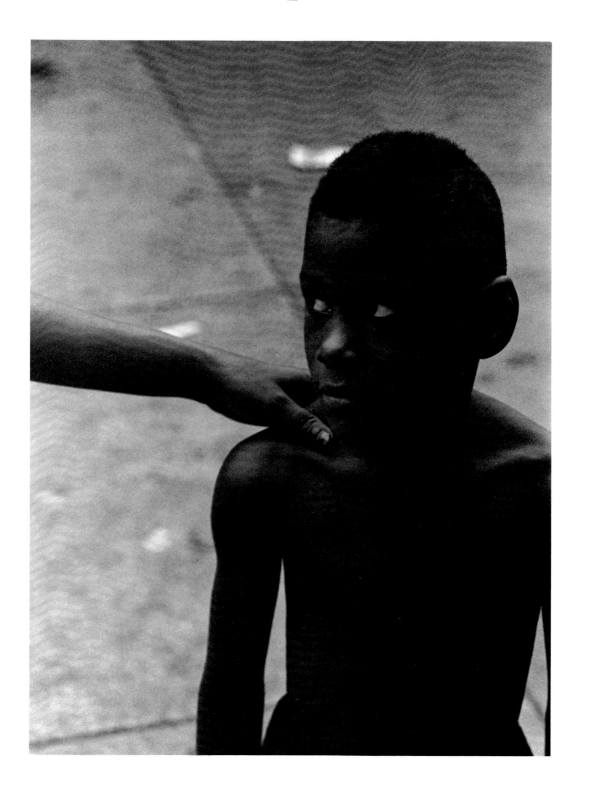

ROY DECARAVA

Untitled. 1952
13⁵⁄₁₆ x 10⅛ inches. Gift of Walter A. Weiss

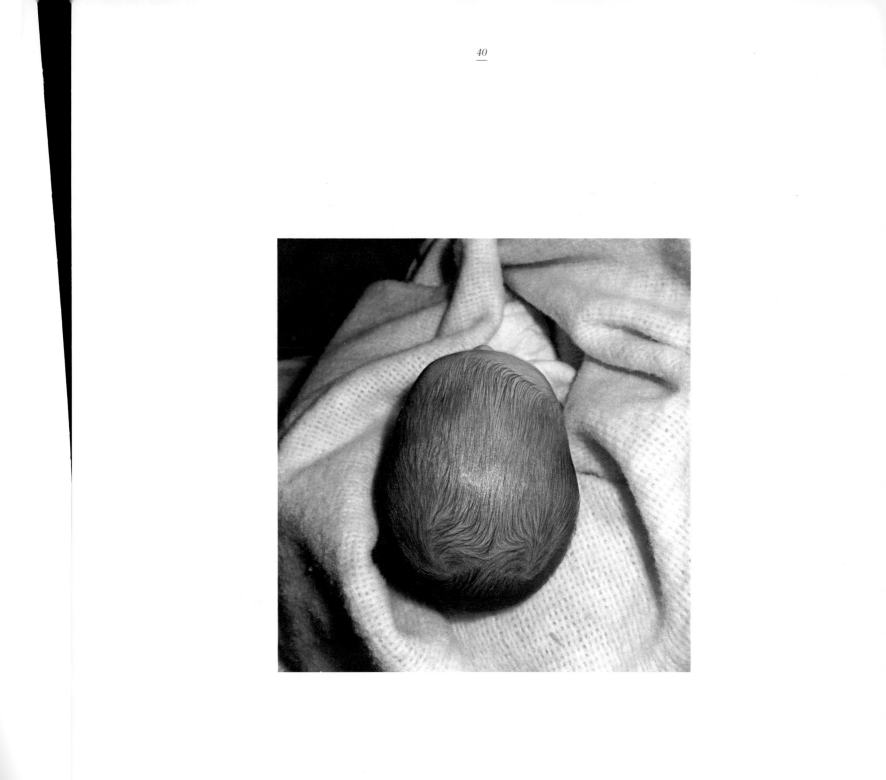

HARRY CALLAHAN

Untitled. c. 1952
7⅛ x 7 inches. Gift of the photographer

JEROME LIEBLING

Boy and Car, New York City. 1948
6⅛ x 5½ inches. Mrs. Charles Liebman Fund

ESTHER BUBLEY

Clinic at St. Luke's. 1951
9⅛ x 12¾ inches. Gift of the photographer

ROBERT FRANK

Pablo, New York. 1958
9½ x 13¾ inches. Purchase

WILLIAM KLEIN

Dance, Bensonhurst, Brooklyn. 1954–55
11 x 14 inches. Gift of the photographer

LOUIS FAURER

Untitled. 1949
8½ x 12¾ inches. Purchase

HELEN LEVITT

113th Street, New York. 1940
8⅝ x 5⅞ inches. Purchase

HELEN LEVITT

New York City. 1940
6⁵⁄₁₆ x 8¹³⁄₁₆ inches. Purchase

DOROTHEA LANGE

Mother and Child, San Francisco. 1952
9⁵⁄₁₆ x 7⅜ inches. Gift of the photographer

HARRY CALLAHAN

Eleanor and Barbara, Chicago. 1954
6⅞ x 6¾ inches. Purchase

SID GROSSMAN
Chelsea, New York. 1938
7⅛ x 5¼ inches. Gift of Mrs. Miriam Grossman Cohen

RUSSELL LEE

Boys learn to garden in vocational training class
at the Farm Security Administration Workers Community,
Eleven Mile Corner, Arizona, February 1942
7½ x 9⅝ inches. Courtesy of the Library of Congress

DOROTHEA LANGE

Damaged Child, Shacktown, Elm Grove, Oklahoma. 1936
10³⁄₁₆ x 9⅜ inches. Purchase

BEN SHAHN

Interior of Ozark School, Arkansas, October 1935
7½ x 9¾ inches. Courtesy of the Library of Congress

RUSSELL LEE

Two children of John Scott, a hired man,
living near Ringgold, Iowa. January 1937
6⁷⁄₁₆ x 9⅝ inches. Courtesy of the Library of Congress

JOHN GUTMANN

Street Boys and Graffiti. San Francisco, 1937
10⁷⁄₁₆ x 11⁷⁄₁₆ inches
Acquired with matching funds from Samuel Wm. Sax
and the National Endowment for the Arts

EUGENE BUECHEL, S.J.

Martha May Fish with an Armful of Pets. March 22, 1931
Modern silver print by David Wing from the original negative, 1975.

EDWARD WESTON

Neil Asleep. 1925
Platinum print, 5⁵⁄₁₆ x 9⁹⁄₁₆ inches.   Extended loan from the photographer.

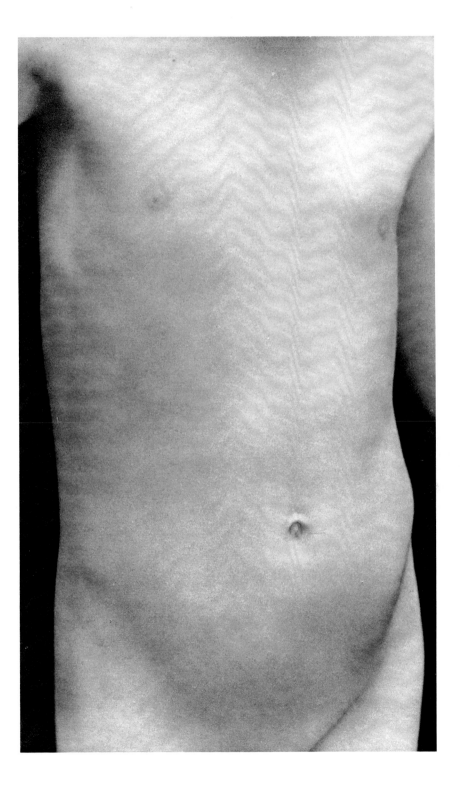

EDWARD WESTON
Torso of Neil. 1925
Platinum/palladium print, 9⅛ x 5½ inches. Purchase

DORIS ULMANN
Portrait of a Young Boy. n.d.
Platinum print, 8⅛ x 6³⁄₁₆ inches. Purchase

LEWIS HINE

New York City. 1912
4%16 x 6½ inches. Stephen R. Currier Memorial Fund

LEWIS HINE

Waco, Texas. 1913
4⅝ x 6⅝ inches. Stephen R. Currier Memorial Fund

CLARENCE WHITE

Miss Grace. c. 1898
Platinum print, 7⅞ x 5⅝ inches. Gift of Mrs. Mervyn Palmer

CLARENCE WHITE

Nude with Baby. 1912
Platinum print, 9¹¹⁄₁₆ x 7¼ inches. Extended loan from the Estate of Lewis F. White.

PHOTOGRAPHER UNKNOWN

Alice E. Foh (?), Age 7. 1860
Ambrotype, 2½ x 2 inches. Purchase

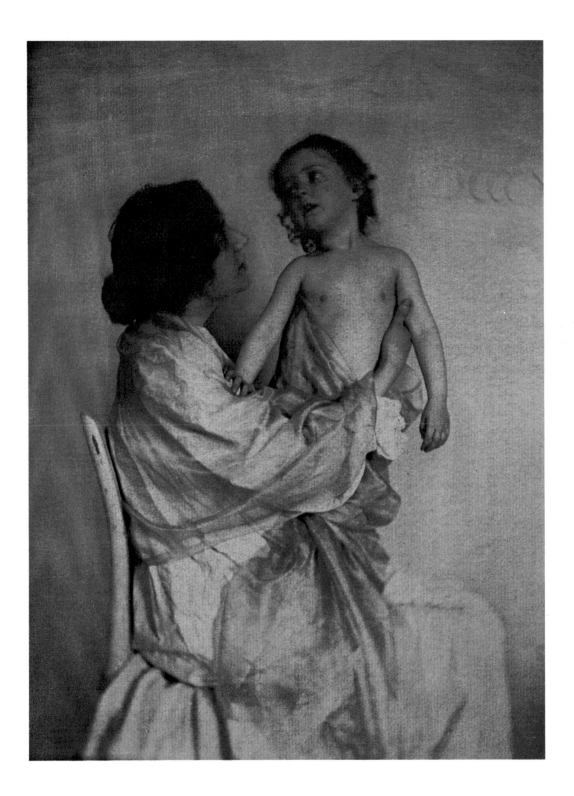

GERTRUDE KÄSEBIER

Adoration. 1900
Gum bichromate over platinum print, 8⅞ x 12 inches. Gift of Mrs. Hermine M. Turner

JACOB RIIS

Talmud School, Hester Street. Early 1890s
4¹¹/₁₆ x 6 inches. Courtesy of the Museum of the City of New York

FRANCES BENJAMIN JOHNSTON

Saluting the Flag at the Whittier Primary School
From *The Hampton Album,* 1899–1900
Platinum print, 7½ x 9½ inches. Gift of Lincoln Kirstein

ARNOLD GENTHE

Children were the pride, joy and chief delight of the
quarter, Chinatown, San Francisco, between 1896–1908
9¾ x 12½ inches. Gift of Albert M. Bender

EVA WATSON-SCHÜTZE

Ben and Bijan. n.d.
Platinum print, 8⅟₁₆ x 6⁵⁄₁₆ inches. Purchase

JOHN G. BULLOCK

Young Anglers. 1896–98
Platinum print, 8 x 6 inches. Gift of the John Emlen Bullock Estate

All photographs in *American Children* are silver prints, unless otherwise indicated.

INDEX TO THE PHOTOGRAPHERS

All the photographers represented in this book are American, and all were
born in the United States unless otherwise specified in the list below.